a jazz funeral for uncle tom

a jazz funeral for uncle tom

HARMONY HOLIDAY

Birds, LLC | Minneapolis, New York, Raleigh

Birds, LLC
Minneapolis, New York, Raleigh
www.birdsllc.com

Cover art: still from Ganja & Hess written and directed
by Bill Gunn and produced by Chiz Shultz, 1973.
Cover designed by Eric Amling
Interior art provided by Harmony Holiday
Interior designed by Mike Newton

Library of Congress Cataloging-in-Publication Data:
Holiday, Harmony
A Jazz Funeral for Uncle Tom/Harmony Holiday

First edition, 2019
ISBN-978-0-9914298-9-9
Printed in the United States of America

French and Spanish Military presence as it clashed with the presence of West African slaves in nineteenth century Louisiana, inspired hybridized brass bands in the Jazz tradition and the subtly militant expression of joy known as the Jazz Funeral. Large army-reminiscent bands playing warm improvised music instead of battle cries give New Orleans a reputation for being almost as dangerously romantic as Paris, people go there to swoon. People go there to die and be reborn in a metaphysical sense, to rediscover lost joie de vivre. In West African theology, death is not the final curtain of a tragedy it's made out to be in eurocentric interpretations, for West Africans and their descendants, beings are deathless, spirits eternal, and dying properly is as important as how you live, the two experiences are inextricable and spirits who don't cross over in peace and exaltation can get stuck between realms, become the undead, zombies and phantoms. Music is the vehicle used to ensure one's proper passage into the next phase of existence and Jazz Funerals are celebrations that employ tone, rhythm, and frequency to heal and release the spirit from the body of the one who has passed. They are large, communal celebrations full of laughing and singing and healing music, and essential to black life in the region. The catholic and protestant churches tried to ban the practice of Jazz Funerals, because in the absence of an alienating sense of sorrow toward death, so-called mourners possess agency and hope, harness enough power to transcend feelings of wretchedness in this life, and generally such defiant black joy is policed in America unless it's arrived at in the service of the established order of things, as entertainment or Christian exegesis. The Jazz Funeral tradition endured nonetheless, primarily among poor blacks, or those who refuse to be coerced into worshiping another culture's gods and observing another culture's rituals. These events are call and response-based so that the communication between attendees mimics communication with the spirit making its passage into the next realm and guiding our survival here. Brass bands and family and friends of the deceased and emancipated spectators with no relation join in the streets with the spirits for muses and make a home of music and commune with transitioning souls directly, and send one on.

Better to leave here alive than to leave here dead — Sun Ra

If I'd had my way I'd have been a killer — Nina Simone

Ask I how do I fly — Lee Perry

A place to be glad

Afro-asiatic   spastic tickle in my throat   when I   go for   it   did you   know there's sugar in the ocean   tangled like slow laughter in the weeds ?   Did you unload   the gun   or remember   a shard of coral calcium   and   send a trance yawning for sunny mirrors before it lunged into your artery   a clearing   either way you're gone   I want to be honest   I celebrated I danced   on   the blunt glass of your nectarine attitude and   sipped   the bloody mud packs of my own deliberate footprints along the way,   fasted on   that blood   until you came back   and my throat   constricted in a two-faced seizure of hope and   dread.

Resurrection is petty   a hustle   a   hassle I love you   I'm so   glad

Uncle what are you listening to?

The Black and Crazy Blues

Dizzy, Run

Tombe lentement vers la   terre   Fall slowly toward   the   earth you've been
sent back to repair   yourself   Stravinsky's virgin   has   returned to
dance   herself   into   eternity and   we all outta jump   back   and kiss
ourselves   feel lucky in the swell and shuck of Ellison's elegant déjà vu   we all
thought   about   leaving   just   to seize in the grandeur of return   to   no-
tice something   new about the space   between   the two front   teeth   of
queens   on the altar   posing   as wall. Keep hearing flutes   and Lucca,
heard your very own daughter   had to sue   you to see you   brought
before   the US Supreme   Court   two blue bloods: a widow and a
child   divvy up Tunisia while a   worm erodes   that eager dimple of yours
beneath the cold wheel of Karma   makes   a   road   makes   a stray   makes
a   traveler   makes   another daughter of dust pushing an empty stroll-
er   across the onramp   Why   are   there   so many men in the sun
pushing empty strollers   from the Salvation Army   so many   ghosts   in
their roll up   on   and   supplies   ponderous devastation the highest highs
are for the fallen   your indented cheek   tastes like   the shed   skin of   gnats
your trumpet   fat with   maggots   your widow fat with greed your se-
cret baby 40   and Ma a fa on her knees helping   her gather the last
of you   and make it say her name

How's it sound?

Beautiful, come from around

Afeni, Run

He kissed the glass, I kissed the glass. Jasmine Guy had an appetite for the quiet witnessing
of it, of our pitiful affection. We had the bridled reluctance of trial day. We read Jean Genet
aloud together   fools that we are   and as radiant, his dirty mouth arousing rejoice and Roy
Ayers   again. The flowers were rude slabs of bamboo and Sambo. And in that sterile else-
where we planted a mayor/ a mother/ a whole way club of sugar and rage. I could see her
cracking open with cyanide and favorite child dope— apple, apple, that rope again, and no
spine in the bell, screaming, I can't kick this when it hits, whispering   it's a boy, nigga, get me
out of this satin ribbon chokehold   alive

What happened to sanity ?

Have you seen the new NASA baby tees at Urban Outfitters. The clerk said she couldn't listen to Bad and Bougie anymore and turned on some Pearl Jam while I bought you yours.

Is it niggas is redundant or niggas is superfluous? What's the difference? It's here comes the whistle man. Hear his call to chaos? You say he enacted a series of reversals, turned his rage orderly, bossy, sloppy-wannabe-mafia/hush? Is it what the hero refuses to do in each situation that leads to further action? There is no hero. The hero is the experience. One woman's willingness to trust her own experience even if it seems at first like a weakness, a series of provocative situations negated by the calling up of conventional emotions. Fake sonorities. Glee as it fumbles into too much leadership. Joyless bureaucrats. We soon discover that the central question is who are we and what are we doing to ourselves? It takes years and years to turn the men real again. What causes it to rain when there are no clouds? Do they disappear to become permanent? And sometimes they become permanent to disappear? And all the middle men show up in love with her willingness to trust her own experience? Yes, and they all say the same patient, let's open our own club someday. But can't we forget all that for now and just play? I am playing all of these niggas. I am singing/ always.

What do you mean by naive relief?

I left a note on your dresser (goodbye
ol' sleepy head)

The bodies just above my head

Crunch, nickname for the other black Christopher, was in charge of the Green Book, less pamphlet that instructs which hotels and roads and restaurants brothels cinemas houses out houses,   etcetera, were safe for crow blacks. Those of us traveling southern back-roads were usually preachers, gospel singers, union men, or entertainers at a time when black entertainers were leaving the Christian church for less regulated and yes more commercial forms of artistic expression. To get paid. To get laid. Danger on the road let us practice our improvisa-tion. The ghosts were real but so were the songs we invented to warn them of our counterpower, soul, which is what they were after, which is why we were in so much danger. Imagine being born without a soul. Or not knowing how to call it. And then you hear Black Christopher sing the urge to hurt him is erotic and retaliatory, he proves your emptiness and leaves you longing for some-thing you are told to despise, blackness, darkness, the higher and higher flame of the original self. Some respond with awe and affection, but entitled affection, the kind that feels like it believes it's doing you a favor, like it's being part of the audience is somehow civilizing, the end goal. We follow this wayward band that reminds us of Sam Cooke from his Soul Stirrer days, we follow them from Harlem to the Deep South, from the halal lchicken stand to the Church Picnic in Birmingham, and we just want them to get where they are going. But we know there's a lamb among them. We know there are corpses in our fairy tales, that all our fairy tales turn to fables in the American South. One of these four traveling singers lilting hymns from the emptied pulpit will have to vanish like a sacrifice into the lives and bodies of his brothers. So when Crunch steps outside to make a call from the phone booth beside the chapel they've just performed in, and disappears, it's almost a relief. But I still find myself wondering how it happened. Where they buried his body. How the Klansmen in that town settled on him as their victim. How he felt being touched by their sweaty hands. And when Crunch's friends gave up the search, the police in the town uncooperative, the citizens too, Crunch's body was always just above their heads, an exit door they didn't know ted looming with shame and promise. It's like this. It's really this way. If you look up. If you hold your head up high, the gash if idle ghosts   the stark pitch of his cry for help transmuted into   a hovered calling   almost halo of   nobody in particular black forms   stretched to gold disaster kneeling in a tantrum   of helpless peace

Did you see any sea lions or
copperheads in the pasture ?

Not the snakes, but I saw a trine of IUDs and
these women celebrating the hold up   blood

Arpeggiated Octave

A yellow rope around the neck of a confederate soldier's statue is so satisfying like they had us imagining his lynching in amber and crow black when he sang or begged for love strangled everyone who lied And when the stone man is tucked into dirt and we cheer promise not to miss the anger promise love is rage and murder is forgiveness this time

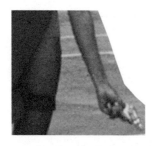

What species of denial was it?

Violins and Meme Sufism

And I could not be diminished

Whenever I start seeing the serpent's translucent spine in the lines separating the vague hemispheres of the fallen leaves from swaying to sinking. Whenever the helicopter is kettle bells. Whenever the bells aren't brooding their rebellion or circling scenes. Whenever the rebel broke the sun   and you come inside   fumbling for resonance   filling me with child. There's a total zipper on the hummingbird's heart.   She is in color, cardinal red   while you beckon in black and white and regressive tethers of   quartz.   Whenever my skin   is that   light's invasion   crowded with the grace   won by   states of total blindness to the   way demolition   men   trade headlines in snowglobe   timing. Something is always falling   in a wallowing spiral so which road is up. And you touch it. Which touch is love   and you know it   by   the   struggle to be righteous   that it   breaks in   you, ends, the evil it condones. Whenever   I'm   feeling   as evil as bliss and as   inevitable   as those presidents   stuffing the bullets of hope   It's brick outside and you're   still a dope fiend   I'm   not coming   to your   rescue this sea- son   is for dancing   to vintage Bjork while   the   sky rivals   hell in its beauty and all   the   sew-ins and lace frontals   of the universe   dismantle   into   sit-in afros

Uncle what are you   brutalizing?

The tom toms   the Black Forest Blues

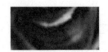

Oriana Felicci, Run

Okay, you are the gospel   you   are   the   gospel   sit down.   If I   lived
here   thinking   like I think, would   you have   me   killed?   How?   They
stopped force feeding   the hunger strikers   I overheard one   choking   on   air   or imag-
ined bicycles that rode him home   when   his   organs   started   to   fail   and fire   tore
a hole in the   wall   That   billowing cowl neck   sweater   that   wilting   ledge
leads   nowhere   step off and   know   you're there   by the terror of ar-
rival   If I   promise you   you   are the gospel will   you spill   primrose
on   my   soft spot   where   the   narc   rocks   itself   woke   spotted   pig
got a lot of   patrons   and poker faces   in   the   window   If I lived   here
looking   like   I look   would you have a   taste?

In what season   do   we   decide that   being   eaten   is   a better   fate
than   being   craved   If I lived   here   talking   the   way   I   talk
would   could   you   save   me   from   the   homicidal   rage   of late em-
pire   using   desire   alone what would my   persona sell for? Would I have
to   taste the Henny on   his   tongue   or razors emerge from   the grass when
I run?   If   I lived   here   as you   desire   would you have   me
stripped for parts like that one Chevy-hearted mischeif?   Thrown   in   a   cell
where   I'd   build   a   railroad   of   omens   while   you   go to   hell?

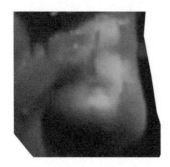

How's it   sound

Sorrowful   come   from   way   down

Kipling-esque

You can't do anything right. Your curiosity is violent. Your empathy is false. Your sympathy is offensive. Your apology is primitive. Your music is sick with envy. Your muses are sick with lust. Your limp doesn't lean. Your straight line is a wink. Your whimper catches December ditching homeroom and only then realizes you stole somebody's name. Your sister brags about anal on the first date. Your reprimand is an amp pumping meth into the trunk. Your clamour is at Wal-Mart. Your brothers hustle codeine. Your table is covered in mugshots and cocaine. You love the way we taste. You ate my daddy. Grind his bones into free rides daily. Then he was on your sweatshirt on the first day of school. You are a pig. You are the slave. You are why I'm yellow. You ate at Waffle House on purpose. Your arrogance is how I'm turning gold. Maybe I can rescue you from your myths about yourself. Maybe I can hide your cadence and break your name into mine. Maybe I can convince you to hand over your children on Sundays and I'll teach them to worship Orishas who each one looks like me. Maybe I can teach you to fear your dreams. Unless they are about everything coming true after death. If you are decent, if you obey me, if you say sorry or please every time I see you smiling, if you let me show you what civilized people do when they are being conquered, raped, ruined, if you let me borrow your heart, if you rip out your own heart and plant it inside me and then eat your bloody hand, if you let me beat you from that central territory and walk through the actual broken glass of my area code to watch me take my father to the grave. The one you ate. The one whose blood you tasted. The one who holds your hand. The one who made you into your brutal savage self again

What happened to joy?

Have you seen the grown ass men wearing store bought camo like they just joined the US Army as remote control slaves? Have you seen the patriots masquerading as poets? All of us?

Justin Bieber and the Lonely Niggas

A lighthearted opus on race violence featuring the TMZ classic one less lonely nigga one less lonely nigga one less lonely nigga one less lonely nigga one less lonely nigga one less lonely nigga one less lonely nigga he said if I kill you there's gonna be one less lonely nigga and then he giggled and then he went about his business making hits

Why do we hide?

Ask I why do I hide

The strife that occurs in the space between two fantasies*

One foot advancing directly in front of the other makes a lasso reeling the black self into the no where else that capital destiny mimics heckles

John Coltrane blows me kisses in that gutted if history so deliberate these days like wave caps

The fingertips drip ribbons and brittle streamers in the elbows' robotic lift the shoulders hustle down modest whole body high on amphetamines mind leaning into the comedown with vulgar reluctance

So I sigh backwards to drink his rotten air

With madness a swingset appears and is as much torture device as pleasure tassel rusted chains that make the palms that grip them smell like blood which reminds us we must be some metallic clutter in the vein of the earth ourselves some constant source of dread and beauty

Now John is throwing bricks like the degenerate alter-ego of someone I love

He practiced until there was blood on the reed and still sounds like a lamb who believes really knows he is a tiger like a trans a trance a rambling wish to die in the middle of the song he is the middle of

If the same   man blowing you kisses is the same man throwing you bricks you can lift   the curse of exertion we've   been to Alabama still can't outswim the phantom and for instance is no way to launch a revelation but something exceptional happens between leaping off the swing and landing in the mud or in the quicksand   or sanity isn't much consolation nowadays

Now he's spitting his grill into the muted leather and we lay our hearts in the shed   alongside the buckling limbs of wild innuendo been dreaming again been watching my hands in the dream so pretty it's almost mean

* from Fred Moten's Black Kant lecture

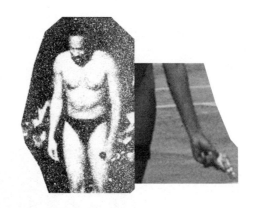

Delilah is hideous

Privacy is hideous

Gilead too   deliberate   who   said
the wounded wanted to be whole?

Save Me / My hands in the dream

In the transition from having an idea to being it   In whatever raid   deliverance
is   In the lifted apathy that becomes defiance on impulse   In the   back
seat with   the tinted windows she was selling the bad seed of
that idea   and there were stacks of cards and empty boatfuls of whis-
ky and that other shit the hipsters love made   from a mexican fungus and
fizzing ulcers   the only way to help any of this is to see it for
what it is to hiss at   the graveyard to think at the yardstick   what
am I even measuring   what is the data of love   and black entitlement
I know I own   everything   I know the land is mine and I'm the land
and my naturalness this candid vision   is why I'm giving it all back
and will not fight any longer to be toxic   and a coward and an American
and that doesn't even mean I'm leaving   I am swinging my feet I am thinking
ahead

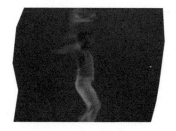

Uncle what are you dancing to?

Duke's Other Side of the Tracks Blues

Prize Fighter

Please tell me that's not a mask on your teeth attached like a jacked up accord-ian I punch him in the eyes and wild orchids bloom

Damn, have any Trap

                              Horace Tapscott or   kicking Horse
                                    Asprin a day   music ?

Gregor Samsa, Run

As greedy as Lou Reed to reach the plateau in a weeping monotone did we? Mumbling through it as if we have to stop talking to keep from eating butterflies and the gloaming is a wall of parlor moths lopping from mouth to mouth to let the cargoed lovers kiss until they share a nervous system, mutation, a good day to do the Moonwalk in chains, they soften, they nearly amuse the hunted when danced off in soft hungry sobs. You'd be surprised how erotic helplessness is. You'd be disgusted with the blank leverage of giants and Mariah having to decide what to kill to appease another resurrection. We are the ones who woke up in new bodies on our backs in those cubbies blinded by cataracts from lack of sun and sending messages to one another through the talking nerves of the spotted moths that thawed our blood from wool. And it's false to assume that we regret ourselves and roam toward some chivalrous disappearance that is convenient for everyone. We wait in the last body before nature to obliterate everything passive or too sane to be real gravy beer sweetmeats bitcoin blockchain neat love plain tough love Brother Tuff's love for Arthur Russell fairweather Garveyism — if the ego survives you didn't kill off your character or keep him alive right just kept him hostage in his phony negritude for a vile eternity and you know what happens to half-assed martyrs who try to come back as movie stars

I have that library card music
that stale Ravel tented Valium Pilgrim n nem
Arch of Bones and Dewey Redman
discourse on methods for   shredded corset

Medgar, Run

Move   beyond the drama of the   light.   And it's got   to be   righteous.   Imagine the sun
coming in through the front door in doved lines of adrenaline   is a catwalk for the damned.
Remove every last piece of flannel and formal cotton and idle toward that hungry sunshine with
knives for eyes. Cut it open. Go inside. You're headed toward your killer, your wife and daugh-
ter are watching and you can't remember if they're in front of you or behind you. Do you protect
them with your body or wave with frantic masculinity don't shoot   these are friendlies. Your
nakedness there doesn't feel obscene and it isn't. The barbarism of a lifetime of ready-made
cloth flashes before your walking porch and you let the regret hang so low it breaks its shallow
edge and becomes the image of you in the blind doorway nude as   page. If this is the first
and last time you will know your body before it's seized by the state   what do you want to
go away noticing: the color   or the shape or how it's shaped by everything near
every idea   every shudder of rage   and love or the feel of the last earth air hitting
your swaying roots with the curse of hope for pleasure   the final arousal soaked in blood
and leisure. Be ready   when they come to kill you, stand on your porch and salute the
dream   the flag   the shooter,   don't haggle for mercy or cover your body in robes and
worry,   terrify them with readiness   make them send you home remind them
who's in   charge

Uncle when are you gonna run?

Never, nigga, the hunt comes to me if I dangle my
appreciation here like a bleeding gash   don't
look   so   sad   that wound that currency

that preacher statue   Julia   ululate   pace
and   toss   me   brave   ones

Heroin and Carrot Juice

You know how we do
petit-dejeuner for petit bourgeoisie negroes and who else swallows ice the light
blue way while humming The Temptations idle in the sandbox camera in the bright rock
playing cops and robbers it's a lot of veins left a lot of checkered Vans looking
plain dandy range rained out hopscotch level lot of vanity in pretending you wanna
save somebody with yo thirsty ass but we believe you so well you know you're in
danger when your lies start to work like rivalries and white weddings question your
safety question your taste

Get Your Respect in Diamonds

But don't you become everything you imitate

Respectable, useless, a saftey net of dark matter in the coke
head's settlement path, cuckolded, wrathless with obligation

ladylike, Ike loved Tina, all is fair in love

Alvin, Run

We no longer have to obey the song   but we have to make it   crave   us,   to be the miss-
ing black notes. There are careful notches of   tape and flour on the floor where your
toes   go   and you have to learn to ignore   them.   There are laws about who gets to be
this beautiful and   all of them you've broken   somewhere   between   hostage and
fugitive   they filled you with the   sickness of   their doubt   they taped your   feet
together and   called   you a heathen under their breath while   kissing you in pub-
lic   a yellow   actual   superimposed on your   bruised knuckles   and   scabbing
and   pussing   and   a stack of maps on   stage with   fake   stars   in the   lavender
lights   and shy freckles on the mic so grotesque   those captains   the whole   choreo
today is to walk onto   the   stage   feet in chains   audience   patient   as   shady
milk   a   room full of expired faces   trying to taste you   and   whispering yes into
tinny palms when the tongues long   for black salt and   honor   just tear the maps to
pieces   with your bare shredded back   facing the blank milk   the funny thing
about surveillance   is they will watch you do anything   pay for it too   geo-
tagged ass brutes   we here   we might   even   love you

Lately, but that could change
like the law

When has the law ever changed,
Uncle?

The Black Capitalist Manifesto

Niggas wanna test the quicksand by dipping their crusty toes in it on a very
ashy day and then call you a witch when you hand them a jagged
stick to climb and shout you aren't the only adventurer so
much time wasted trying to prove that hell exists it'd be faster if you'd
just up and go there with yo eclectic taste having nirvana meets sade loving
ass with yo miraculously jaded forest of agate bling and rich homie quan
astrophysics code switching ass with yo it's all in the mind/so what ass with
that picture of my ass in your back pocket like prayer with yo cab callo-
way showtunes cane wielding ass with yo wondering if david blaine is black
or just strange magic is to tragic as deep thoughts on a shallow day ass
it'd be so much faster if it's speed you're looking for gutted method

personally I'm after the drastic quickening that occurs when something
disappears and yet remains what is a body what is a vessel what is another boat
and another what brought us over where did it go the getting over where
did we hide the quietest covenant and like that paper like that in god
we trust behavior that buys me all these prophetic grapes seedless
but still a deep purple still searching for the caress of teeth and mumbling croco-
diles and dilated for the rave and costumed and collapsing in a map of black salt —
Preservation Hall Jazz Band is gonna march out from the wings and start
playing the theme song now Migos' Walk It Talk It for big band and a
hologram of the Jackson 5 boys! Children! Can it be we stayed away
too long it can't be that But I have to confess I celebrated with yo
arrogant enough to test the haunted waters ass with you naive enough to
make dead ass popular slang for when you're being true with yo sooth is
a youthful mood ask me now then it was per-
sonnel now it's personal

Never, but all unnatural laws shall
        be   broken,   crossed

Are you one of the ones who
needs to come undone to
come together ?

Just this Once

It was around this time she was seen traveling with books of negro spiritu-
als reporters invade the sacred with the desperation of conspiracy every-
day she chanted wake the children sleeping and wished for his disappearance
everyday he returned. Dorothy Day or Bresha Meadows the blows the
puzzled winds of the chosen keep a record for them. When the
time arrives like a message watch out for them. If you're brave enough to
sleep beside the woman you've beaten watch out for them. And so the
child of 14 entered the quiet legacy and shot her father in the head
while she gently slept. And so the nest is no longer a cage but may-
be a graveyard. And maybe it's fun to watch a monster die and see your
father again with his new eyes, how she healed him crying it's so nice
to watch you die. America, this is your dream come true. This is your
perfect Meadow this is your first black president Bess is your woman
now confessing and everything real never fraudulent and as
for selling expectations And as for shameless silhouettes and blood
wet whispers in the new sirens and as for her protected future and
her Reparations and her Ruins

Did you steal some plums and run away from home?
Did steel cut oatmeal make you feel boatless and symmetrical?
You still don't know what love is?

Kamasi, run

When you go this way   you   can go on forever   girasol to   the heart and rose cov-
ered converse   not even an overdose in   the   hinge   and   the canvass of misremem-
    bered   history no longer restricted to the tv in the attic   what style! What black
latitude passing   jessie owens on the way to cairo, no   longer   having to snitch to tell it
no longer abracadabra relic shit   or the broke down credibility of edges   or the
    Rexall with the   arcade   in   the   back   where they   sold   the last battle   Mu-
hammad Ali would walk in trembling   his daughter on his arm to help keep him upright
that's our prize fighter that's   the   other ruins the rented body of a champion
warning you   to stay seated until you're   called   on   and now you're   called
on   and caught running through the streets screeching   caught leaning into pitch-
  es with Willy Mays   caught between   a   yesterday's   reflex   and   today's
that   place   where ambivalnce finally leaves   no   traces   unstruck   un-
restrictricted   dangerous to   quit if you   go   this   way   you must
                                                                    go   on

                                                                    forever

Uncle I want you to get
          some rest

          I want you to get arrested and turn
          into Malcolm X   or get restless and
          disappear like Hess did or just play
          east of yesterday

Coin Coin, Run

Damn son   he   grunted   holding his   falling   jeans and   sprinting sideways in
high hay   and concatenation   He didn't   want   to chase   the   favor
he hadn't   planned to live forever   he didn't   know   he had a fever   thought
it   was   a   true love shopping spree   thought   the cotton needle   was   a
vaccine   thought   the   visine   was   tiny   water   and   the   eye   a re-
liable   bank   in   the space between   seeing   and   being   seen   and
plenty   quenched   and   hesitant and   addicted   to fickle sonance   and espio-
nage   fake Prada   real   caught   up   ketchup packets spilling from   his   pockets
Dexter   Gordon   flickering   in   his locket   on   grin   on   roar   on dim-
ples   and   porridge   this   is   your   typical   roll   out   strategy pretend   to
shift   into   helpless   chaos   and   laugh   when   they   fall   for   it   such
tall   grass   in   ol miss   such that   mystery of the body   of   the   boy   of
the   ball   is   leaping   violently   into   pinstripes   he   was   isolated
yes   but   he   never   made   us   nervous   he   never was   convicted   he
never took   that   back pack   he never made it to Rikers   he   never   did
come   back

I can't see nobody
I can't see nobody

The blackbird singing or just after

Then I noticed on the anniversary of your death this cheerfulness how proud I am of a voyager a seer I overheard the guy with ash between his eyebrows and Prince's former assistant who now works at my local crystal dealer liberate empo- rium I go in for cinnamon incense and to test my intuition and drink this grapefruit/cayenne juice in the comfort of a telegraph they were discussing what happens when a bullet enters the flesh how it's not the impact that hurts but the gunpowder searing your inner organs burning them on contact the flame once lit leveraged as potential like all trauma the sentient ram is mostly calm as a smirk in the aftermath slower than everything happening clearer de- serted river banks becoming mirrors the finger you shot off has never been didactic never wagged never asked for the nerve back had the nerve to know better to grow a palate there a dialect new flesh I'm so proud of you mom told me the news the day after valentine's day in grand- ma and grandpa's hallway in stucco san diego everything so clean and so quiet you could hear the clock's constant ticking and crickets and the grass- hopper that landed on my shoulder and smiled she told me about a new place you had travelled to and then collapsed sobbing I'm so proud of you you're so jubilant and dignified on the other side with Ruth and Elijah and some brides and your love higher and high- er the cut of the last scream is laughter it was like we were in two different places hearing two different stories while she wept I gathered the openest pleasure in my eyes the deliberate calm of retreat the ecstacy of nevermind I'm so proud of you so proud to be of you so happy for you so through with sadness so new and ruthless   and   you and   Ruth   and   Elijah   and all   the   distant cousins and

all   the   bloody gloves   and all the loose myths about   all   of   us   and

the   way you sing save me   like Nina Simone does and really   mean   it   and

really   prove   what it means   to   build a bridge   to walk   the muted wa-

ter   I'm so proud   of   the   proof of   you   the bruises   healed   the

comfort came   all of our effort turned into ease   the wounds went

away   or went blind or ran off on other cinder   but   the songs   are

still   here   it was ash Wednesday in   the   year of our lord anno domini

something or other   Prince died on my birthday Nina Simone too   I love

tribes   I like   that late April   makes people feel safe to take   off to slay   the

stiff lion   that looms in the yard with   the lemons and Ma a fa just learn-

ing   her name and the deacon and   the lot we bought in Atlanta and

tips of tongues skipping like   pamphlets   we don't need communism   any-

more we don't need to sound smart about dumb shit we don't   need to

do   crunches in a paded cell I'm so   proud   of   you I'm so full

of truth and   hours   thank you for going over there   for being here   and

there   for the new grass for   the magnetic tape   and the way stitches

disappear into skin like the quick indigo grin of morning   you make me

proud as all disappearing you set me free as a near intention   you ask me

to sing about it too now or teach me or through me so proud

I'm so   proud and how

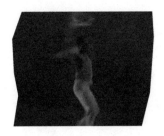

Uncle where are you?

Uncle what are you leaving to?

#metoometoometoometoometoometoometoometoome-
toometoometoometoometoometoometoometoometoome-
toometoome

the meat and music   the wound and tune   method   the
chase method   butsomedaysIs-
itandwishIwasakidagain

A Paradise of Ruins

You know I cuddled with gardenias and an obelisk at the club   waiting for Lee Perry's
magic matches. The cinder twitches with ignition and the flattened ark is   a   ruins
and the last ditch is a bridge and the new one is no one   pitching planks
in the lungs   confessions hungry theories of how evil   that land becomes
without ocasional torches   and borderline psychotic urges to throw them into
Rendition   And so he did   and not the least bit listless   burn his own
palace into myths   and if you can get in line with the myth the re-
ality has been abolished   and   if you can do that black the   world
had ended and he was twirling in the embers   a madman
and tender rampage of flesh my dennis rodman my abolitionist my
ab workout dub soundtrack you cannot have this royalty and not lead
with irreverence you cannot bleed in purple and not know how to
call it like one swallowing the last of your drugs in line at
the airport the fool in you is conspicuous, jittery giggling at nothing
and so beautiful a jury and so urgent in his search of something to
ruin to prove that we were here   but it won't be a woman this
time it won't be ma wounded in your locket of rhymes and that evo-
lution in the loose gums of the newly dead and nearly god got him
weary with excitement thinking about all the fights he could win with
himself against himself and a little slack in the the flower shoulder-
ing her last ear reverberated with go head on

Uncle who do you love?
Nobody but us?

What could a coward do for hero   besides
go   to hell   which was   the   next
song

What's Funny?

But unfortunately, he never lost his way   jaded   hawk   leaking   off   beat
playful lark in heap of museum   styrofoam   objective transporta-
tion from   black lungs in coal country   to black longing in   stolen brass
he found it in a taxi   my hot comb bandit and the   picture
of Eric he carried and pasted on hotel walls   don't be
afraid don't be alarmed   there's no more karma there's no
greater charm in good behavior than in murder include the
faceless machine   dress for a post human planet play some
music (I'm talking to the disc of google robot, she listens) let's see
what she's gonna play let's trust an invasion of fate again
and again an obsession with the mescaline ziplock swarovski zip-
lock what would zukovsky or tristen do she plays Frank Ocean's
Biking the robot does a dose a follow close The Gift of the Black Trop-
ics is not wheels but slow slow braiding in a field on Sun-
day blunt remembering and Paul Mooney's shimmering renuncia-
tion   the ghanaian olympian dancing in his sled red yellow and
green tepid oblivion isn't an option   and the hot nothingness
of the song singes indifferent flesh into   shadow

I have to admit   I   celebrated

What could a hero do for   a   cow-
ard   besides   carve   of   ruins
                 a   reclaimation

                                    you wrong for that   back   and
                                    forth   in   a vacuum of side-
                                    eye   chorus

And you consider yourself virtuous ?

I've eaten the gold dutifully   in   fistfulls   heard   him all   laughing in the heart of the Honduran rainforest   on   night when the   lotus blooms, passing through me in caves and echo   so   that I   reach the white of   his   teeth and hang on   dangle in my   ligaments   'til those blanched seeds rot and   regrow   as the petals   that wheel   the   road   to   divine   hunger: punch drunk   punch drunk I murdered him before the catchers could   kill him, an act of love/disdain. Once again: adrenaline.   Have you ever tried to   step past   the dream into   eternity   and   realized there is no   border   between   will   and   desire but love of ache's rapture   this talking cage tree   and the things you go searching for   to   break   his   fever must be the same ones   that brought it   on   smiling   obnoxiously into greedier glass while   he   giggles   like he's beating the brains out of someone he   remembers   keeping him just alive and vivid enough to do it   again   tomorrow

Is this tomorrow?

Afterward

I've long glorified and helped sustain the defensive, huddled, hyper-masculinity that the West invented and bestowed upon many black male archetypes in the place of other clout or perceived power and credibility. I've loved violent (deflecting), rude (hyper-sensitive), pathetic (restless), beautiful (obsessive), genius (nervous), willfully dumb (dumb), two-timing (one mo gin), lying (pathological), cheating (fake), self-deluded (afraid), overblown shadows of men with vivid self-abnegation, but I didn't always see it that way. Maybe I still don't. To be jaded is too lazy, not in me, because everything I've loved, I've been, or longed to be, to conquer, either to kill it in me, to obliterate it completely from the face of anything I'm observing, or to arouse it and leave with a slow ruthless parade float wave in my deliverance. A blatant carnival, the carnage of misapplied power as it rescinds and redistributes itself. And anyways a savior complex is more about the call to adventure than some wallowing or docile generosity, though the masquerade is never really over, though it's a little of both, because we're taught that the boldness of the martyr is more virtuous than the audacity of the endlessly curious adventurer. But there comes a time of vicious decampment, of naming things into anonymity, of regaining the childlike curiosity in meanings without any confusion about the use-value of reclaimed language and behavior, a new attitude. And that time arrives around the same time you realize that all your real heroes are dead and you've been trying to resurrect them through your own suffering of real-life fools and how's that working out for you? It's around the time you learn all the dead and hagiographed personalities were human once too. Because it's then that heartbreak is no longer romantic, it's finally real and difficult, liberating and sacred, and so with heart broken open by every failed revolutionary impulse that causes the ones you long to love to recoil into puppets, there comes a time to bump a few imposters out of the spotlight of your mind, to create space for new heroic actions, to face the aromantism of anything less than revolution and reparations, to question everyone's stamina and taste and commitment to beauty and truth, especially my own. What had been so alluring about domineering mostly broken men? What had been so true about backing their endless private tantrums with the glory of my exquisite attention in fact or in fantasy? Why had I been reluctant to lay these Toms to rest and get on with the real important tasks? I guess distractions and false obstacles are good excuses to defer one's own call to duty. Either way the charade of being captivated by empty charisma gets boring, finally. I think a lot of women have reached this stage, where as painful as it is to realize we have to take it from here, we know that it's up to us to do something different, to look on from a new vantage, to change the way men behave by changing the way we regard them and ourselves, really looking again. And there is no greater love than that which is willing to rename you over and over until you are the many, no longer the shattered unreconciled one. The love that gives you new places to hide, provides new forms of refuge, while at the same time stripping you of disguises. In the process, the feminine is often just numbed into chorus, but not in this case, the event at hand, the adventure here, is the clearing of the way for our epic heroine, the last adventurer before nature, by laying Uncle Tom and all admiring onlookers to unapologetic, rest, laying down the burden of a restrictive fantasy. And how do you defend yourself against a fantasy?

spent her final years working as a maid for a white woman despite having devoted her life to diligently collecting all of the grunts and snorts, shrills and moans of his stupefied condition, in the fields, on the corner, at the counter, from the ceremony, to the hound den, the same man who found his own voice so pretentious he only whispered or screamed, couldn't work the middle, has passed into the next part of his journey, died in his sleep while on a plane fleeing to Paris. Uncle Tom was born into slavery but earned his freedom dancing as a stripper for his white slave mistresses, they offered tips and pet his head until he felt as ready as a beast or an adulterer for his nightwalks. Freed, he moved to Eatonville and later to Chicago then Boston, where he made his living as a tailor by day though he never stopped selling to the white women, it was a bit more dangerous for a free man than it was for a slave, to be touched by the other race. Sometimes he missed the certainty of the whip, and he often beat his wife Julia with the good leather belt he had lifted from a deceased customer. That felt healthy and as close to love as he'd ever be, beating the black off the mother of his seven children. Uncle Tom had wanted to be a good man, the best kind of man, a faithful, deliberate, and always home on time kind, but he lost track of who and what to be faithful to and self disappeared in the losing of that. Mirrors were cruel and ever wide and descriptive of a bible and a broken field hand hiding in the scripted factory. Uncle Tom became a rapper after his first son ran away to live back in South where the cotton crumbled into women who could cook grits and shoot guns. He felt something stolen that only language could return or demand in currency. He felt like a stowaway in a bang up song and wanted to rewrite his hunted lingering. Uncle Tom became everything he thought about and he thought a lot about a house, about a stethoscope, about the road, about the joke in the song that became that hook that he then hung from, clapping. Uncle Tom was ridiculous, the greatest pretender. He couldn't disagree with anyone, he never knew Duke Ellington from Monk from Andrew Hill from Cousin Mary, he didn't want to recognize any difference between souls, and as bitter as this futile refusal made him, he smiled and tamed his will to recoil into a position on the lantern's edge. Watchman. Sellout. He had so many disguises and all the cadillacs and pinstripes to match. A couple cardigans, hard dimples and soft socks, shamrock and ciroc. Free Meek Mill. Free the people, free the land. We mean it. And Mumia, and the mummies stolen from Egypt and on display in some museum in England. Uncle Tom is a burning wish; he is a wish that burns eternal. He is a songbook purged through rehearsal, one who must be practiced to be destroyed, loved into uselessness, and then at last, gone.

**Harmony Holiday's
100 Favorite Jazz Recordings**

Sun Ra
God is More than Love Can Ever Be

Billie Holiday
Strange Fruit

Nina Simone
Wild is the Wind

John Coltrane
My Favorite Things

Sun Ra and June Tyson
The Satellites are Spinning

Bessie Smith
St. Louis Blues

Charles Mingus
Haitian Fight Song

Miles Davis
Bye Bye Blackbird

Miles Davis
Petit Machins

Miles Davis
Bitches Brew

Miles Davis
Solea

Dizzy Gillespie
Cherokee

Ornette Coleman
Eventually

Eric Dolphy
God Bless the Child

Booker Little
Man of Words

Phineas Newborn Jr.
All the things you are

Abbey Lincoln
Tender as a Rose

Andrew Hill
Love Chant

Betty Carter
Something Wonderful

Alice Coltrane
Translinear Light

Pharoah Sanders
Upper Egypt & Lower Egypt

Billie Holiday
God Bless the Child

Dorothy Ashby
Afro Harping

Mingus
Meditations on Integration

Nathan Davis
Suite for Martin Luther King

Amiri Baraka
Black Spirits Intro

Stanton Davis
Ghetto Mysticism

Doug and Jean Carn
Spirit of the New Land

Max Roach
I Had the Craziest Dream

Donald Byrd
I often heard my mother cry

Cecil Taylor
Nefertiti, The Beautiful One has Come

John Coltrane
Stellar Regions

Phil Cohran
Malcolm X

Mary Lou Williams
Black Christ of the Andes

Thelonious Monk
Crepuscule for Nelly

Thelonious Monk
Solo Piano

Art Blakey and the Jazz Messengers
Orgy in Rhythm

Tony Williams
There comes a Time

Billie Holiday
'Tain't nobody's business if I do

Tony Williams
A Famous Blues

Rahsaan Roland Kirk
Brightmoments

The Bobby Hamilton Quintet
Dream Queen

Duke Ellington
In a Sentimental Mood

Bill Evans
Conversations with Myself

Charlie Parker
A Night in Tunisia

Miles Davis and Gil Evans
Porgy and Bess

Duke Ellington
Sacred Concert

Miles Davis
So What

Herbie Hancock
Empyrean Isles

Bobby Hutcherson
Now!

Max Roach and Abbey Lincoln
We Insist! Freedom Now Suite

Horace Silver
Song for my Father

Amiri Baraka
Come Back Pharoah

Charlie Hayden
Liberation Music Orchestra

Charles Mingus
Moves

Charles Mingus
Myself When I'm Real

Charles Mingus
Taurus in the Arena of Life

Don Cherry
Codona

Sun Ra
Springtime Again

The Descendants of Mike and Phoebe
A Spirit Speaks

Nat Adderley
Quit It

Wayne Shorter
Speak No Evil

Booker Ervin
Cry Me Not

Billie Holiday
There is No Greater Love

Steve Kuhn
The Meaning of Love

Muhal Richard Abrams
Young at Heart/ Wise in Time

Freddie Hubbard
Red Clay

Nina Simone
Don't Smoke in Bed

Joseph Jarman
Black Paladins

James Moody
Moody's Mood for Love

Jose James
The Dreamer

Elvin Jones
Agappe Love

Duke Ellington
Haupe

Rahsaan Roland Kirk
The Black and Crazy Blues

Dexter Gordon
What's New

Woody Shaw
Blackstone Legacy

Billy Harper
Capra Black

Billy Parker's Fourth World
Freedom of Speech

Hampton Hawes
Universe

Gabor Szabo
Dreams

World's Experience Orchestra
Beginning of a New Birth

Clifford Jordan
Glass Bead Games

Rahsaan Roland Kirk
Prepare Thyself to Deal With a Miracle

Mal Waldron
Black Glory

Roy Brooks and the Artistic Truth
Black Survival / Sahel Concert

Muhal Richard Abrams
Levels and Degrees of Light

Stanley Cowell
Brilliant Circles

Archie Shepp
Yasmina, A Black Woman

Yusef Lateef
Like it Is

Ahmad Jamal
Extensions

Oliver Nelson
The Blues and Abstract Truth

Lee Morgan
Search for the New Land

Eddie Gale
Eddie Gale's Ghetto Music

Sun Ra
Nuclear War

Archie Shepp
Mama Rose/ Poem for Malcolm

Archie Shepp and Philly Joe Jones
Howling in Silence

Hannibal Marvin Peterson
and the Sunrise Orchestra
Children of the Fire

Cecil Mcbee
Voice of the 7th Angel

Billie Holiday
Baby, I don't cry for you

Horace Tapscott
Dem Folks

George Russell
*Electronic Sonata for Souls
Loved by Nature*

Billy Strayhorn
Lush Life

Harmony Holiday is a writer, dancer, archivist, director, and the author of four collections of poetry, *Negro League Baseball*, *Go Find Your Father/ A Famous Blues*, *Hollywood Forever*, and *A Jazz Funeral for Uncle Tom*. She founded and runs Afrosonics, an archive of jazz and everyday diaspora poetics, and Mythscience, a publishing imprint that reissues and reprints works from the archive. She worked on *S O S: Poems, 1961-2013* by Amiri Baraka, transcribing all of his unreleased poetry recorded with jazz which only exists on primarily out-of-print records. She is now editing a collection of Amiri Baraka's plays. Harmony studied Rhetoric at UC Berkeley and taught for the Alvin Ailey American Dance Theatre. She received her MFA from Columbia University and has received the Motherwell Prize from Fence Books, a Ruth Lilly Fellowship, and a NYFA Fellowship. She is currently completing a book of poems called *M a à f a* and an accompanying collection of essays and memoir *Love is War for Miles*, both to be released this fall, as well as a biography of jazz singer Abbey Lincoln. Her work is deeply rooted by Black music and collective improvisation with Black people, in the tradition of her father who was a Northern Soul singer and songwriter and introduced her to artists he worked with like Ray Charles, The Staples Singers, and Bobby Womack.